Louisiana DWI Guide:

"How to Survive a DUI Arrest" in New Orleans, Jefferson Parish, St. Tammany Parish, Baton Rouge, Metairie, Gretna, Kenner, Covington, Slidell, Houma, and all other Louisiana Cities and Parishes

by DWI/DUI Defense Lawyer Stephen Rue

Copyright © 2017 Stephen Rue

All rights reserved.

ISBN-13: 978-1541379541
ISBN-10: 1541379543

Louisiana DWI Guide   www.StephenRue.com

DEDICATION

The Louisiana DWI Guide is dedicated to the lawyers and staff at Stephen Rue & Associates who work diligently for our clients.

Table of Contents

Introduction: What You Need to Know — 10
Chapter 1: Why DWI is a Serious Charge — 12
Chapter 2: What Could Happen to You? — 14
Chapter 3: Louisiana's DWI Law — 16
Chapter 4: The DWI Traffic Stop and Initial Police Investigation — 19
Chapter 5: Field Sobriety Tests — 26
Chapter 6: Preliminary Breath Testing — 47
Chapter 7: Your Arrest and Bail — 52
Chapter 8: The Secrets to Hiring an Experienced DWI Attorney — 56
Chapter 9: Your DWI Defense — 61
Chapter 10: To Plea or Go to Trial — 67
Chapter 11: The Louisiana DMV and Your Driving Privileges — 68
Chapter 12: Clearing Your DWI Record — 75

Selected Louisiana DWI Laws are found at: www.LouisianaDWILaw.com and www.StephenRue.com.

Important Information from the Author Attorney Stephen Rue:

Disclaimer: Please note that all of the contents in this book is intended and provided solely for informational purposes and to educate the reader. This book does not provide legal advice to the reader in any actual case. The information in this book does not create a legal attorney/client relationship with Stephen Rue or the law firm of Stephen Rue & Associates, LLC. The attorneys at Stephen Rue & Associates may provide actual legal advice upon a direct and personal consultation which can be arranged by you calling (504)529-5000 or (985)871-0008. As each case involving an arrest for driving while intoxicated (DWI) or driving under the influence (DUI) has specific and different facts underlying the case; thus, each case must be reviewed and analyzed on an individual basis. Likewise, Louisiana law is dynamic, and changes do occur. The laws may have changed since the publication date of this book; therefore, you should contact a competent and experienced DWI Attorney to advise you of any current changes in the law that may affect your case. Additionally, we have provided selected Louisiana DWI law on our website at **www.LouisianaDWILaw.com**.

If you have been arrested or charged with a DWI, DUI or related crime or traffic offense, it is important that you do not exclusively rely on the information in this book; you should immediately contact a competent DWI criminal defense attorney to assist you. Please note that the information in this book does not create a legal attorney/client relationship with Stephen Rue or the law firm of Stephen Rue & Associates, LLC. If you wish to retain Stephen Rue & Associates, simply contact us for an appointment by emailing us at Rue@StephenRue.com or by calling **(504)529-5000** or **(985)871-0008**.

Likewise, your state driving privilege's may be detrimentally affected if you fail promptly to request an Administrative Hearing. This is a separate proceeding apart from your DWI arrest. There are time deadlines that affect your rights. Please immediately contact Stephen Rue & Associates or another experienced DWI attorney for assistance and actual legal advice for your case.

About the Author Attorney Stephen Rue:

Stephen Rue is a very experienced DWI attorney who has a tremendous support team. He and his legal team which, includes a former Assistant District Attorney who previously prosecuted hundreds of DWI cases, has over 30 years of intense experience in representing persons charged with First Offence DWI, Second Offense DWI, Third and Fourth Offense DWI, and related serious traffic related offenses throughout Louisiana. Stephen Rue and his other experienced attorneys are available to assist you or a loved one in criminal defense representation. Stephen Rue & Associates have several offices throughout the Greater New Orleans Area, including New Orleans, Gretna, Kenner, and Covington. Call to speak with Attorney Stephen Rue at (504)529-5000 or (985)871-0008.

Mr. Rue is a highly-respected trial lawyer, author, and lecturer. Stephen Rue is honored by being selected the **"BEST ATTORNEY"** in Gambit Weekly's Best of New Orleans Readers Poll (2012). Rue was selected for inclusion within **"Louisiana Super Lawyers 2017."** Stephen has a **"SUPERB" 10 out of 10 Rating by AVVO Attorney Ratings**; Rue received the AVVO Client's Choice Award in 2014 in the field of Criminal Law. Stephen Rue is honored by **the National Trial Lawyers Top 100 Lawyer Award for 2016 Criminal Lawyers**. Rue received the National Association of Criminal Defense Attorneys (NACDA) **"2015 National Ranked Top Ten Attorney Awards for Excellence in the Field of Criminal Defense."** Rue is also honored is honored by receiving the **National Association of Distinguished**

Counsel's (NADC) Nation Top One Percent Award in 2015. Rue is a 2017 member of the **American Association of Premier DUI Attorneys**. Stephen Rue continues to receive many 5 Star Yelp reviews from his clients. Stephen Rue is a **Fellow of the National Institute of Trial Advocacy**. Rue has lectured to associations, attorneys and law students on issues regarding various trial litigation skills and techniques. Stephen Rue's awards and invitations to membership in prestigious legal organizations grows yearly.

The esteem most appreciated by Stephen Rue is that received by the praise of his clients. You can review his client testimonials at his law firm's websites at **StephenRue.com** and **LouisianaDUILaw.com**.

You are invited to contact Attorney Stephen Rue and his team of experienced attorneys at **(504)529-5000** or **(985)871-0008.** The telephone is answered 24 hours a day, seven days a week.

Client Testimonials:

"Stephen Rue's law firm successfully helped me through a very difficult time. Their legal expertise and personal attention to my case made all of the difference in the world. Thank you. Thank you. Thank you."
- DWI Client, New Orleans

"I received a third-offense DUI. I did not know what to do. Thankfully, I called Mr. Rue's law office. They took me through the process, and I felt protected to the entire time. I highly recommend Stephen Rue & Associates."
- DWI Client, Jefferson Parish

"This was a serious DUI and I was facing serious charges, and I knew that I was in trouble and could lose my job and spend time in jail. My attorneys Stephen and Larry worked very hard to protect my rights and resolve the matter without me losing my job or my freedom."
- DWI Client, St. Tammany Parish

Please note that individual results may vary. For more Client testimonials, please go **to www.StephenRue.com**

Stephen Rue & Associates Law Firm:
An Experienced Approach to DWI Representation

My name is Stephen Rue. I'm an attorney who represents folks charged with DWI and other related traffic offenses. I take my job very seriously, and so does my legal team dedicated to your justice and working hard to ensure that you don't get unfairly taken advantage of by the legal system. The truth is that not everyone who is charged with DWI is guilty of DWI. There may be an insufficient basis for the police to make the initial vehicle stop. The law enforcement officer may have been flaws in made errors his suspicions of intoxication. There are many viable reasons that someone could have red eyes and not be able to recite the alphabet backward under stress. There may be many inaccuracies in the field sobriety tests. No everyone can walk a straight line and touch their nose fully sober, including many law enforcement officers. The breathalyzer test may be inaccurate and register a false refusal. The breathalyzer machine may be inaccurate and not calibrated correctly. The law enforcement officer may not be certified to operate the breathalyzer machine. There may be errors in the police officer's reporting of the stop, testing, and arrest. For these reasons and much more, you want a trusted well-known competent attorney who has vast experience dealing with DWI cases. You need an attorney who can surgically review your case and take the appropriate actions that are best for you.

Introduction:
What You Need to Know

In **The Louisiana DWI Guide,** you will learn why DWIs are considered so serious in Louisiana Courts and throughout the Country. We will discuss what could happen to you.

We will inform you as to what you should know about Your Traffic Stop and the Police DWI Investigation. We will discuss the actual arrest and bail. You also will provide suggestions on how to hire the right DWI attorney. And discuss winning defense strategies used by very experienced DWI lawyers. You will also learn about Louisiana DWI law, penalties, and fines. Likewise, we will discuss your driving privileges and whether your driver's license will be suspended and what to do about it. This guide also discusses the possibility of a civil suit if the drunk driver is in a car wreck. We also will discuss expungements of DWI public records.

Your best moves in surviving a DWI arrest is to become informed and prepared and learn how to hire a Louisiana DWI lawyer for your case.

"Driving While Intoxicated" (DWI) and "Driving Under the Influence" (DUI) are used to reference the crime of operating a vehicle while intoxicated or under the influence of drugs (Louisiana Revised Statute 14:98 and related law). We generally shall use the term of DWI as it more commonly used by the public in this State. To review the Louisiana DWI laws, please go to www.LouisianaDWILaw.com

If faced with a first, second, third or subsequent DWI arrest, the first best move you can make is to ensure that it does not happen again. Please do not drink and drive or drive under the influence of any drugs that affect your ability to drive safely. Secondly, you must hire a very experienced and competent DWI litigator who can assist you in making the best decisions and implementing the best defense strategies to protect your rights and freedom.

Chapter 1

Why DWI is a Serious Charge

Few people expect to get arrested for Driving While Intoxicated (DWI). For most folks, when it happens, it comes as a real shock and becomes a real eye-opening experience. Most people arrested for DWI are otherwise law abiding citizens The DWI arrest becomes a devastating life event that often makes one reflect on their life choices. God willing, no one was injured or killed as a result of the drunk driving incident. Unfortunately, the truth is that many tragedies do occur.

Let's start off with the truth about Driving While Intoxicated and Driving Under the Influence. Drunk driving creates tragic consequences. Approximately twenty-eight (28) people die from drunk driving accidents each day. Every two minutes, someone is injured by a drunk driver or someone operating a vehicle while under the influence of drugs. Every 51 minutes, someone's loved one dies from a DUI crash. In 2015, 10,265 people were killed and aroundfessional Conduct Committee 290,000 were injured in drunk driving accidents. Astonishingly, this represents approximately 31 percent of all traffic deaths. The National Highway Traffic Safety Administration (NHTSA) estimates alcohol is a substantial factor in nearly half of all motorcycle fatalities. Recently, there were 7,977 DWI/DUI arrests in Louisiana. This is precisely why Louisiana courts and judges take your DWI arrest very seriously. The concern is amplified by the ongoing presence and monitoring of organizations such as Mothers Against Drunk Drivers (MADD).

If you have a substance abuse problem, then please to seek appropriate counseling, intervention, and treatment. If you or a loved one is impaired, please don't operate a vehicle. Ask a sober driver to take you home. Take a cab, Uber or other means of third party travel; and please be safe and sober.

Many drunk drivers believe that there is a good chance that they will not be pulled over by a law enforcement officer. If they get in a wreck or get pulled over for DWI, then many people end up at my law office.

This book was created with the understanding that all of us do not condone or endorse driving drunk or impaired. We do not. *What we do advocate is that everyone is entitled to Constitutionally mandated due process and fairness in the judicial process. A competent and experienced defense attorney can assist you in that process.*

Chapter 2
What Could Happen to You?

It has been our experience that many of my new DWI clients that come into our law office are law abiding citizens who are gainfully employed and have little or no prior encounters with the police. My clients generally are fearful of going to jail, losing their job and hurting their finances, damaging their reputation and injuring their future. A wise decision is to hire the right DWI attorney who has extensive experience dealing with DWI cases in the parish of the DWI arrest.

As stated in Chapter 1, in Louisiana, Driving While Intoxicated (DWI) is a serious offense and can have life-changing consequences. Louisiana DWI's are punishable by imprisonment, probation, fines and costs, driver's license suspension and may include other requirements of the Court such as attending mandatory Alcoholics Anomalous (AA) or Narcotics Anonymous (NA) meetings and providing numerous hours of service with community service programs.

When you have a pending DWI charge, you will not be able to rent a car, your insurance rates will likely significantly increase, a conviction could affect your job and career, and should you hire an attorney, there will be the cost for your attorney.

After your arrest, your name may end up in the newspaper notifying the community of your DWI arrest. Any DWI conviction will be on your public record, subject to your attorney getting the conviction set aside or expunged. Law

Enforcement agencies will always be able to review as to whether you were convicted of a prior DWI. If you receive a second or subsequent DWI, your penalties can be substantially enhanced and increased. It is important to know that a third offense DWI in Louisiana is a felony.

Also, the court can mandate installation of something called an Interlock Ignition Device (IID), which prevents you driving unless you blow a sober breath into a device. Those penalties all likely sound intense – but it's not even the full picture!

Other situations can complicate your DUI defense. For instance, if a drunk driver is in a car accident, the drunk driver may be sued in civil court for general damages and potential punitive damages.

The truth is that not everyone arrested for DWI is found guilty of driving while intoxicated. Everyone is entitled to a competent defense that may get the charges dismissed, diverted, reduced, or mitigate the damages in a plea bargain. Some DWI convictions can be set aside and expunged off of the public record.

Some cases require a trial to determine innocence or guilt. The State of Louisiana has the burden of proof. There are many ways in which a competent DWI lawyer may increase your chances of a more favorable result, dismissal or acquittal. After you read, we would love to learn more about you and your situation and provide a FREE consultation about your next steps. (Please see the end of this book for more details.)

Chapter 3

Louisiana's DWI Law

Let's look at Louisiana's DWI law to get a basic understanding of the offenses associated with operating a vehicle while intoxicated or under the influence of a controlled dangerous substance.

In Louisiana, Driving While Intoxicated (DWI) and Driving Under the Influence (DUI) two general descriptions used by the public and attorneys for the state crime of <u>operating a vehicle</u> while <u>intoxicated</u> or <u>under the influence of drugs</u> (referred to in the law as "controlled dangerous substances").

Louisiana courts have considered **"operating"** a vehicle to include driving, moving, parking, sitting in a vehicle with the engine running, and other instances where there is some element of "control" of the vehicle. A competent DWI attorney will evaluate whether there is an opportunity to disprove the "operating" element of the offense.

A **"vehicle"** includes motor vehicles such as cars and trucks, as well as aircraft (planes and helicopters), watercraft (boats and jet skis), vessels and "other means of conveyance." A "vehicle," for purposes of Louisiana

DWI law, does not include a bicycle or a horse.

"While Intoxicated" refers to one's physical state or condition at the time of the alleged operation of the vehicle subject to the DWI arrest. Under Louisiana law, the "intoxication" does not have to be what is commonly referred to as being "drunk." Rather "intoxication" for purposes of DWI law refers to being under the influence of alcohol or drugs and/or having a blood level concentration (BAC) at or above the applicable legal limit. If a driver is over the age of 21 and has a BAC of 0.08% or greater, then that individual is presumed to be "intoxicated" for purposes of Louisiana DWI law. For a driver under the age of 21, if there is a BAC of 0.02% or greater, then that individual is presumed to be "intoxicated" for purposes of Louisiana DWI law. Besides intoxication by the consumption of alcohol, a driver may be charged with DWI for being under the influence of certain drugs that affect one's ability to operate a vehicle, whether legally prescribed medication or illegal drugs.

In Louisiana, First and Second Offense DWIs are misdemeanors. Third and subsequent DWI's are felonies. As more fully outlined in this book, the costs and penalties associated with a DWI conviction are greater the potential jail time, fines, administrative fees and court costs found in the law.

DWI laws will change over time. It's best that you have a competent DWI attorney explain the current law to you. You may review the Louisiana DWI laws for First, Second, Third and Fourth and Subsequent DWIs (Louisiana Revised Statue 14:98 through 14:98.8), Underage Driving Under the Influence, and applicable laws for refusal to take chemical tests as our website www.LouisianaDWILaw.com.

Other serious crimes related to driving while intoxicated or under the influence include vehicular homicide, vehicular negligent injuring, first-degree vehicular negligent injuring, child endangerment, and other related crimes. These are likewise found at www.LouisianaDWILaw.com.

When arrested for DWI, a driver also faces suspension of his driving privileges. Please refer to Chapter 11 of this guide.

Chapter 4

The DWI Traffic Stop and Initial Police Investigation

The vast majority of DWI arrests originate from a law enforcement officer pulling over a driver who he suspects is operating a vehicle under the influence of alcohol or drugs. In other instances, a DWI investigation begins when a driver is in an accident, in a parked car or is no longer in the vehicle. In those cases, the police usually follow varied investigation techniques which you can discuss with your DWI defense attorney.

Talented DWI attorneys often file motions to suppress evidence obtained at the initial encounter traffic stop based on a constitutional challenge of facts surrounding the stop.

Law enforcement officers must have a constitutionally accepted justification to detain a driver under the Fourth Amendment to the United States Constitution. This Amendment to the Constitution protects against "unreasonable searches and seizures" and requiring "probable cause." The Courts have determined that mere initial communication and interaction between a citizen and the police implicate no Fourth Amendment concerns where there is no coercion or detention. Likewise, The United States Supreme Court has ruled that, upon the reasonable suspicion, supported by specific and articulable facts, a police officer may briefly detain an individual if the person is suspected of having engaged in criminal conduct. The A driver suspected of DWI cannot be arrested unless and until the officer has "probable cause" for a custodial arrest.

If you were pulled over by a police officer while driving, police would look to driving cues in their initial observations to determine if someone is driving under the influence of alcohol and drugs. A driving being pulled over and temporarily detained and interrogated foe suspicion of DWI, which must be supported by a factual basis, is generally called an "investigatory stop." This is the beginning of the investigative process of the law enforcement officer to determine if you should be arrested for DWI.

Drivers operating a vehicle while impaired frequently exhibit display certain effects or symptoms of impairment including slowed reactions, impaired judgment, impaired vision and poor coordination.

The law enforcement officer's first job is to determine whether a driver in intoxicated or under the influence of drugs. The police officer has a secondary role to collect proof of intoxication or impairment. This "evidence" is collected through the officer's physical observations of the driver, through the officer's opinions based on field sobriety tests, through chemical testing, driver statements, video/audio evidence, and witness testimony.

In a standardized arrest for a non-accident related DWI, law enforcement officers typically follow as a checklist to help am officer reduce or minimize mistakes in the DWI investigation, arrest, and subsequent narrative DWI Arrest Report. This very same checklist can be used by a competent DWI defense attorney to look into areas where there may have been flaws, errors or inaccuracies in the police investigation and arrest.

These areas of are as follows:

- Whether there was "Reasonable cause" in the "Traffic Stop."
- Facts surrounding the "Traffic stop."
- Officer's "Approach" to the vehicle
- Officer's "Introduction" and statement of reason for stop
- Officer's securing of Driver's license, insurance, registration and other documents
- Officer's initial observations
- "Pre-Miranda questioning (Before reading of constitutional rights against self-incrimination)
- Field sobriety tests
- Preliminary Breath Testing
- Warrant for Blood Testing, if applicable
- Blood Testing, if applicable
- Officer's "Conclusions" as to driving while intoxicated or impaired
- Arrest
- Post-Miranda Questioning (After the reading of Constitutional Rights against self-incrimination)
- Officer's continued observations
- Witness statements
- Disposition of Vehicle
- Booking
- Officer's Preparation of Report(s)

The National Highway Traffic Safety Administration (NHTSA) has interviewed law enforcement officers from around the country to accumulate a list of acts that create suspicion that someone is operating under the influence. The factual basis of a reason suspicion of intoxication or under the influence of drugs creates the legal "probable cause" that police use as the basis for the initial vehicle stop. In this study, the NHTSA found over 100 driving activities found to predict that a driver has a blood alcohol concentration (BAC) of 0.08 percent or greater.

The NHTSA interviewed law enforcement officers from across the U.S. From the interviews a list of more than 100 driving cues that are used to predict blood alcohol concentrations, or BAC's, of 0.08 percent or greater, was developed. The four general driving activities that alert police to a potential suspension of a DWI are as follows:

1. Failure to maintain proper lane position;
2. Speed changes and braking;
3. Drivers "vigilance;" and
4. "Poor or impaired judgment."

The chances of being pulled over under the suspicion of a DWI increases substantially when a driver displays one or more of the following activities:

- Swerving and weaving
- Weaving across lanes
- Drifting from side to side within lane
- Straddling the lane line
- Rapid variation of speed
- Excessive fast speed

- Excessively slow speed
- Turning in a wide radius
- Problems stopping or breaking
- Nearly striking another vehicle or stationary object
- Striking another car
- Driving in opposing lanes
- Driving the wrong way on a one-way street
- Driving on an undesignated roadway
- Failure to use traffic signals for turning
- Following too closely to another vehicle
- Operating a vehicle at night without headlights on
- Running stop sign or signal light
- Failure to respond to Police Officer signals and instructions to pull over

Once the police have stopped your vehicle, the law enforcement officer looks for post-stop cues of intoxication such as the following:

- Booking
- Officer's Preparation of Report(s)
- The driver has difficulty getting out of the car
- The driver has difficulty turning the car off
- The driver fumbles for his driver's license or car registration
- After exiting the vehicle, the driver has difficulty maintaining his balance, stumbles or is unsteady in his stance
- The driver has difficulty opening the car door
- The driver fails to take the car out of gear
- The driver leans against his vehicle for support

- The driver has slurred speech
- The driver has an odor of alcohol or marijuana
- The driver has bloodshot eyes
- The driver may voluntarily give an unsolicited statement admitting to drinking alcohol or using drugs
- The driver drops objects in his hands
  The vehicle has alcohol bottles or cans in plain sight of the officer
- The vehicle has drug paraphernalia in plain sight of the officer
- The driver vomits, urinates or has soiled clothing
- The driver acts in a very disorderly manner
- The driver uses abusive language, profanity or profane gestures towards to police officer
- The driver is slow to respond to the police officer's requests

"Pre-Miranda" Questioning

At some point, the police officer that pulled over the vehicle will have personal contact with the suspect and start asking investigative questions which are referred to as "Pre-Miranda" investigation. This means the police officer is asking questions <u>before</u> having a reasonable suspicion that the driver being questioned has been driving under the influence and thus has broken the law.

The questions that are usually asked by the police officer usually include one or more of the following inquiries:

- "Have you been drinking tonight?"
- "Have you taken any drugs today?"
- "Where are you coming from?"
- "Where were you traveling to?"
- "How much have you had to drink tonight?"
- "When was the last time that you had something to drink?"
- "Why do you think I stopped you?"
- "Are you sick or ill?"
- "Are you injured?"
- "Are you being treated by a doctor?"
- "Have you taken any medications today?"
- "Is there anything wrong with your legs, feet or back?"
- "Is there anything wrong with your eyes?"
- If you are in an accident, the office will ask, "Have you had anything to drink since the accident?"

During this "Pre-Miranda" questioning, the officer will be gathering information as to the driver's condition. At some point, if the officer has a suspicion that the driver may be intoxicated or under the influence of drugs, then he may request the driver is submitting to **"Field Sobriety Tests."**

Chapter 5

The Field Sobriety Tests

At some point, if the police officer determines that he does not yet have probable cause for an arrest for DWI, the officer will ask to administer what is commonly referred to a field sobriety tests. Most law enforcement agencies now have their officers equipped with body cameras and their police cruisers equipped with video cameras and microphones. The digital images of the field sobriety tests regularly are used in court as evidence. Law enforcement chooses field sobriety tests to assist in determining whether a driver in impaired sufficiently to be unable to safely operate a vehicle, to establish probable cause for an arrest and to use as evidence against the driver in the DWI prosecution by the State. These tests are used to determine the driver's mental and physical abilities needed for safe driving including testing the following:

1. Balance
2. Steady Reactions
3. Steady Vision
4. Muscle control
5. Coordination
6. Information processing and
7. Short term memory

Field Sobriety Tests generally include a battery of these tests:

1. "Horizontal Gaze Nystagmus" (Eye test)
2. "Walk-and-turn."

3. "One-leg-stand."
4. "Finger-to-nose."
5. Reciting the alphabet
6. Modified position of attention, also known as "Romberg" Test
7. Touching Fingers of hand to thumb and counting with each touch; and
8. Counting backward from a number

All of the field sobriety tests presume that the tests were administered with clear instructions and demonstration and fairly understood by the suspect. Those presumptions should be attacked by a competent criminal defense attorney.

Only three modes of field sobriety testing are considered sufficiently reliable as a testing of intoxication to be recommended by the NHTSA for "**standardized testing**." The NHTSA standardized tests are:

1." Horizontal Gaze Nystagmus."
2. "Walk-and-turn," and
3. "One-leg-stand."

We shall discuss effective and specific defenses used by experienced DWI defense lawyers in Chapter 9.

Horizontal Gaze Nystagmus Test

Testing for horizontal gaze nystagmus is one of a several field sobriety tests used by police officers to determine whether a suspect is driving while intoxicated. When someone is intoxicated by alcohol and/or certain drugs, eye jerking becomes more pronounced. Hence, the horizontal gaze nystagmus test is used by law enforcement agents to evaluate an individual's nystagmus to determine if probable cause exists for a DWI arrest. The eye test involves observation of the suspect's pupil as it follows a moving object while noting that:

1. The eye's lack of smooth pursuit following a moving object,
2. Distinct and sustained jerking nystagmus at maximum deviation, and
3. The onset of nystagmus jerking before 45 degrees.

Nystagmus is an eye condition of involuntary eye jerking movement; that may result in reduced or limited vision. It is often referred to as jerking or dancing eyes due to the involuntary movement of the eye.

Nystagmus may be caused by congenital disorders, acquired and/or central nervous system disorders, toxicity, drugs, alcohol, or simply rotational movement.

The horizontal gaze nystagmus test has been highly criticized by experts and defense lawyers as major errors in the testing methodology and analysis can be found.

Despite vast criticism as to its reliability, the validity of the horizontal gaze nystagmus test for use as a field sobriety test for individuals with a BAC level between 0.04–0.08 percent has been found to be a more accurate indication of blood alcohol content than any other standard field sobriety test.

When an officer attempts a Horizontal Gaze Nystagmus test, he is supposedly testing whether your eyes have a lack of smooth pursuit movement following along with a small moving object, usually a flashlight or pen. There are many flaws with the attempted use of this test which can be attacked by a competent and experienced DWI attorney.

Before an officer attempts to administer the horizontal gaze nystagmus test, the officer should evaluate the eyes to see if there is a resting nystagmus, equal pupil size and equal tracking (meaning both eyes have the ability to follow a moving object together). If any of these factors are found, there is a good chance of an existing medical condition or injury that will render the test unreliable for purposes of determining alcohol impairment.

Legal Challenges to the Horizontal Gaze Nystagmus Test

The NHTSA has established standardized Field Sobriety Test Procedures. According to these standardized instructions, the law enforcement officer is to provide the DWI suspect with the following instructions:

> 1. Please remove your glasses (if worn).
> 2. Put your feet together, hands at your side. Keep your head still and
> look at and follow this stimulus with your eyes only.
> 3. Keep looking at the stimulus until told the test is over.
> 4. Do not move your head.
> 5. Do you understand the directions?"

Your attorney can undermine any flaws in the standardized instructions and the test's implementation.

Even when administered in the most ideal of scenarios, depending on the study referenced, the horizontal gaze nystagmus is only 77% to 96% accurate in determining if an individual is intoxicated or impaired. Not only that, but there are numerous neurological, medical and eyes conditions that could cause the onset of nystagmus—which is something only a doctor, such as an ophthalmologist, not a police officer, could determine.

Your competent Louisiana DWI lawyer should address the fact that there are numerous non-alcohol related causes of nystagmus such as the following:

Regarding the Horizontal Gaze Nystagmus test, there are numerous reasons that are not related to alcohol for someone to have issues with eye Nystagmus. Non-alcohol-related causes of nystagmus can include, but are not limited to, the following:

1. Anti-convulsants
2. Antihistamines
3. Arteriosclerosis
4. Aspirin consumption
5. Barbiturates
6. Brain Damage and Disorders
7. Brain hemorrhage
8. Carbon monoxide
9. Chemical exposure
10. Circadian rhythms of the heart

11. Diet
12. Disorders of the vestibular apparatus and brain stem
13. Dry-cleaning fumes
14. Epilepsy
15. Excessive atmospheric pressure changes
16. Excessive consumption of caffeine
17. Excessive nicotine exposure
18. Exposure to solvents
19. Extreme chilling
20. Eye muscle fatigue
21. Eye muscle imbalance
22. Eye strain
23. Glaucoma
24. Head Traumas
25. Heredity
26. Hypertension
27. Influenza
28. Inner-ear inflammation and problems with the inner ear labyrinth
29. Irrigating the ears with warm or cold water under peculiar weather conditions
30. Korsakoff's Syndrome
31. Lesions
32. Measles
33. Multiple sclerosis
34. Motion sickness
35. Muscular dystrophy
36. Prescription medication
37. Streptococcus infection
38. Sunstroke
39. Syphilis
40. Toxins
41. Tranquilizers

42. Vertigo; and
43. Visual field movement

"Walk-and-Turn" Test

A large percentage of the completely sober population of this Country would be challenged by having to a walk in a perfectly straight line, heel to toe, then pivoting and they do it again. This is one of the three standardized field sobriety test routinely performed to determine if there is probable cause for a DWI.

The NHTSA attests that the "Walk-and-Turn" test has only a 66% accuracy rate—and that's when it is "properly" administered according to their standardized guidelines. This means that as a whole the "Walk-and-Turn" test is 34% inaccurate as a basis to determine intoxication or under the influence of drugs. This is fertile ground for your qualified DWI defense attorney to attack is use, and it's "results."

According to these NHTSA standardized instructions, the law enforcement officer is to provide the DWI suspect with the following instructions for a "Walk-and-turn" test:

1. Put your left foot on the line, then place your right foot on the line
ahead of your left, with the heel of your right foot against the toe of
your left foot.
2. Do not start until I tell you to do so.
3. Do you understand? (must receive affirmative response)

4. When I tell you to begin, take nine heel-to-toe steps on the line
(demonstrate) and take nine heel-to-toe steps back down the line.

5. When you turn on the ninth step, keep your front foot on the line and
turn taking several small steps with the other foot (demonstrate) and take nine heel-to-toe steps back down the line.

6. Ensure you look at your feet, count each step out loud, keep your
arms at your side, ensure you touch heel-to-toe and do not stop until
you have completed the test.

7. Do you understand the instructions?

8. You may begin.

9. If the suspect does not understand some part of the instructions, only
the part in which the suspect does not understand should be repeated.

When an officer attempts a "Walk-and-Turn" test, the police officer is supposed to give these standardized instructions for the DWI suspect to this dexterity test. The instructions are to be accompanied by a physical demonstration by the investigating officer. Your defense attorney should inquire as to the location that the test was conducted and the circumstances in which it was conducted in order to insure ample space was allowed for the test, the ground was level and not slippery, the weather conditions were not windy, what shoes were being w manuals conspicuously state that elderly individuals over 65 will have difficulty satisfactorily completing the test.

Likewise, the HHTSA recognizes that overweight individuals and persons with back, leg or inner-ear problems may also have difficulty with this field sobriety test because of the pre-existing physical impairments. Further, women wearing heels higher than two inches should be permitted by the officer to remove their shoes before taking this test.

The test is often videotaped and used as evidence during the criminal prosecution of the DWI.

While you are participating in the test, the law enforcement officer will look for a number of clues that indicate a blood alcohol content (BAC) level of .10% or higher. These include the following:

- Difficulty balancing while listening to instructions
- Starting the test before the instruction stage is complete
- Stopping while walking, failing to walk heel to toe
- Stepping off of the line, using arms for balance
- Turning incorrectly, and
- Taking the incorrect number of steps.

This field sobriety test is susceptible to numerous avenues of impeachment as to the "results" by your DWI defense lawyer.

"One-leg Stand" Test

The third and last "standardized" field sobriety test is the "One-leg Stand" Test. This test also is used to determine whether a driver has a blood alcohol content (BAC) level of .10% or greater—and if the officer can establish "probable cause" to make a DWI arrest

In order to minimize and reduce the likelihood of mistakes and errors, the investigating officer is to use the following verbal instructions to the DWI suspect, after a demonstration of how to perform the test:

1. Stand with your feet together and your arms at your side (demonstrate)
2. Maintain position until told otherwise.
3. When I tell you to, I want you to raise one leg, either one, approximately 6 inches off the ground, foot pointed out, both legs straight and look at the elevated foot. Count out loud in the following manner: 1001, 1002, 1003, 1004 and so on until told to stop
4. Do you understand the instructions?
5. You may begin the test.

While the test is being performed, the officer looks for several clues of intoxication including the following:

- Swaying
- Using arms for balance
- Hopping to maintain balance, and
- Putting your foot down.

Should the police officer observe two or more of these "clues," then the suspect allegedly fails the test.

The reliability of the One-Leg Stand Test is very poor. Studies have shown that is only has a 65% accuracy rate of determining intoxication when properly administered. This means that on its best day, this test is inaccurate 35 % of the time. Furthermore, your attorney should try to discredit the procedure, instruction and demonstration used when implementing this test.

Non-Standardized Field Sobriety Tests

The three standardized field sobriety tests previously described have been "validated" as more reliable by the NHTSA to determine intoxication.

Law enforcement often also use non-standardized tests of even less reliability and accuracy in determining intoxication. "Non-standardized" testing means that the NHTSA has no formal guidelines on the administration or scoring of the tests. This makes the "results" of these tests very subjective and prone to any inherent bias of law enforcement officers administering the tests. There also is a significant level of statistical unreliability of these tests in establishing proof of intoxication

The standardized as well as the non-standardized field sobriety tests are considered as 'divided attention' tests insofar as they test an individual's ability to take instructions and perform various tasks upon request of the officer.

Non-standardized field sobriety tests include the following:

- Swaying
- Vertical Gaze Nystagmus
- Romberg Balance Test
- Finger-to-Nose Test
- Finger Count Test
- Hand Pat Test
- ABC Test, and
- Numbers Counting Backwards Test

Vertical Gaze Nystagmus

The Vertical Gaze Nystagmus Test is different from the standardized horizontal gaze nystagmus test. When the investigating officer administers the vertical gaze nystagmus, the officer will hold a small object such as a penlight approximately 12-15 inches from the head/nose. With the suspect's head held still, the officer will observe your eyes following the penlight/object with your eyes when the officer moves the object in an up and down vertical motion.

As stated when discussing the horizontal gaze test, there are numerous reasons unrelated to intoxication that could cause the suspect to "fail" the test. Your well informed DWI attorney should attack this test for its numerous innate flaws.

Romberg Balance Test

German Neurologist Moritz Heinrich Romberg created a balance test that evaluates a person's neurological functions. The NHTSA has adopted the use of this test for use in DWI investigations.

The "Romberg Balance Test" test is based on the idea that two of the following three functions are necessary to maintain balance: vision, equilibrium and spatial orientation with a person knowing how your limbs are oriented in space.

To administer the "Romberg Balance Test, the investigating officer requests the suspect to stand with his feet together; head tilted slightly back and his eyes closed. The suspect is being asked to estimate when 30 seconds has passed, and say "stop" when he think it's been that 30 seconds.

While the suspect is complying with these instructions, the officer is evaluating six clues that allegedly may indicate intoxication. These six clues are as follows:

1. Amount and direction of swaying
2. Eyelid and/or body tremors
3. Estimate of when 30 seconds has passed
4. Muscle tone
5. Sounds or statements made during the test, and
6. Ability to follow directions.

As there are no formal guidelines on its administration or scoring of this test, your attorney will have many ways to attack use and alleged "results."

Finger-to-Nose Test

Investigating police officers often use unofficial tests during a traffic stop such as the "Finger-to-Nose Test." Here, the officer requests the suspect to close his eyes, tilt his head slightly back and then touch his nose with his index finger. The officer asks the suspect to repeat this action three times on each hand.

While the suspect is complying with these instructions, the officer is evaluating various clues that allegedly may indicate intoxication.

These five clues are as follows:

1. Inability to follow instructions
2. Swaying
3. Eyelid and/or body tremors
4. Speaking or making sounds during the test, and
5. Failing to touch your finger to your nose

The "Finger-to-Nose" test was for doctors to assess neurological function and motor coordination, not to determine intoxication of DWI suspects.

Finger-Count Test

The Finger-Count Test (a "divided attention" test, as it measures your ability to follow instructions and perform a physical task) is another commonly used <u>non-scientific</u> and <u>non-standardized</u> test used by police officers in their series of field sobriety tests. Studies have been conducted to determine the accuracy of this test.

In this "test," the investigating officer asks the suspect to extend his arm in front of him, with his palm facing forwards. He is then asked to use the top of his thumb to touch your remaining fingers, each time counting each time the fingers and thumb connect. This series is repeated three times.

While the suspect is complying with these instructions, the officer is evaluating various clues that allegedly may indicate intoxication.

These six clues are as follows:

1. Starting the test too soon
2. Having problems following directions
3. Having problems counting
4. Having problems touching each finger correctly and in the right order
5. Having problems performing the correct number of sets of the test, and
6. Stopping the test early.

The Finger-Count test simply is unreliable as a test for intoxication. Additionally, many other physical conditions such as illness, neurological conditions and sleep deprivation could also produce poor results to this "test."

Hand Pat Test

In the non-standardized Hand Pat Test, the DWI suspect is requested to extend one arm outward, with his palm facing upward. The suspect is then requested to place the other hand on top, with the palm facing down. The suspect is then asked to rotate his top hand 180 degrees to "pat" the bottom hand with the back of his other hand and count "one" before rotating it again, so the suspect's top palm touches the bottom palm while he counts "two." The investigating officer will request the suspect to continue to count until asked to stop. Many sober individuals are unable to do this test.

While the suspect is complying with these instructions, the officer is evaluating various clues that allegedly may indicate intoxication.

The four clues are as follows:

1. Problems following directions
2. Starting too soon
3. Failing to count as instructed, and
4. Failing to pat your hands correctly

The National Highway Traffic Safety Administration (NHTSA) does <u>not</u> approve the Hand Pat Test. This "test" can be affected by an individual's normal lack of coordination problems, arthritis, and many other reasons.

ABC Test

Yes, investigating police officers may ask a DWI suspect to recite the alphabet backward. Usually, if this test is administered, most officers request the suspect to recite a portion of the alphabet, for example from "G" to "U."

While the suspect is reciting part of the alphabet backward, the officer is evaluating various clues supposedly evidence of intoxication. The four clues are as follows:

1. Slurred speech
2. Starting the test early
3. Having problems reciting the alphabet correctly, and
4. Difficulty following directions

This a non-standardized test.

The ABC test "results" can be affected by a DWI suspect's nervousness, education, memory, language barriers and outside distractions.

Counting Numbers Backward Test

A final non-standardized test frequently used in an investigating officer's battery of field sobriety test is the "Counting Numbers Backward" Test. The test is self-explanatory.

While a suspect is counting backward, the police officer will look for several clues of intoxication or drug impairment. These clues include the following:

1. Starting or stopping counting too soon
2. Counting incorrectly, and
3. Having problems following directions

Your DWI attorney will have an arsenal of objections to the use and findings of the Counting Numbers Backward Test as have been previously referenced in this guide.

Attacking the Accuracy of Field Sobriety Tests

The alleged "results" of field sobriety tests are subjective. When standardized field sobriety tests were first used and endorsed by the NHTSA in the 1970s, studies showed that they were only 47% accurate at predicting intoxication of a driver. Over time, the NHTSA recommended further procedures and specific questions and demonstration which increased the accuracy of the standardized field sobriety tests to 82 % overall in determining if an individual's blood alcohol content (BAC) is .10% of greater when all three standardized tests were administered. An 18 % error margin is huge when using the tests that affect someone's liberty, reputation, and financial status. Many defense experts and qualified scientists have the strong opinion that field sobriety tests, both standardized and non-standardized, are unreliable indicators as evidence of intoxication.

The NHTSA found that the individualized "standardized" tests had varying levels of accuracy/inaccuracy as follows:

1. Horizontal Gaze Nystagmus Test - 77% to 98% accuracy rate (Thus, a 23% to 2% inaccuracy rate)

2. "Walk and Turn" Test - 68% accuracy rate (Thus, a 32% inaccuracy rate), and

3. "One Leg Stand" Tests - 65% accuracy rate (Thus, a 35 % inaccuracy rate)

The NHTSA itself has questioned the subjective nature and inaccuracy of prediction intoxication of the "non-standardized" tests; that is precisely why it has not allowed those tests to be deemed "standardized."

Field sobriety tests can be challenged and contested based on several factors beyond their innate statistical inaccuracy. First, law enforcement officers who do not administer the standardized tests or grading methods correctly arguably rendering the tests invalid. Additionally, there are numerous physical and medical conditions of the driver that could impair an individual's ability to completet successfully any of the field sobriety tests administered. Many of the physical and medical conditions have been noted in this chapter. Another possibility is that a particular investigating officer was improperly trained to administer field sobriety tests.

Refusing the Field Sobriety Tests

What do you do if you see flashing lights behind your vehicle and you're the person being stopped? You may think to do exactly was is requested of you by a law enforcement officer. However, it is important for you to know that you are not required to perform field sobriety tests.

You Can Refuse the Field Sobriety Tests

As a direct result of known inaccuracies in the actual tests, the administration, and grading of the tests, and the medical and physical non-alcohol reasons that someone would be incapable of successfully completing the tests, the taking of field sobriety tests are not mandatory, and you may refuse to take them. In general, most DWI agree that of an investigating law enforcement officer is asking you to take field sobriety tests, then he likely already has a belief or substantial suspicion that the driver is intoxicated or under the influence of drugs. If so, the officer is seeking further collaborating evidence of the driver being illegally impaired for purposes of establishing "probable cause" for the arrest and use as evidence for the prosecutor in court.

The reality is that if a police officer is asking a driver to take the field sobriety tests, if you politely say no thank you, you very well may still be arrested under the suspicion of DWI; however, the prosecution will not have the field sobriety "evidence" to use against you in a DWI trial.

If instead, you agree take the field sobriety tests and then "fail" one or more of the tests, then the officer will likely then request that you take a chemical breath test, commonly referred to as a breathalyzer test. There are legal repercussions if you refuse to take the breathalyzer test based on what is known as the Implied Consent w which is discussed further in the following chapter dedicated to this subject. Remember that you have the right to refuse the test and a Constitutional right to remain silent and not incriminate yourself.

After the Louisiana police officer conducts these field sobriety tests, he will ask you to take the breathalyzer test.

Chapter 6

Preliminary Breath Testing

Preliminary Breath Testing, commonly referred to a "breathalyzer" provides "evidence" of the breath alcohol concentration (BAC) of the alleged impaired driver. Usually, the driver has not yet been arrested when he is requested to submit to the breathalyzer test. The police generally argue that the suspect is still under investigation.

Taking the breathalyzer test may corroborate or uncorroborated the law officer's initial impressions of the suspect's impairment gained from his initial vehicle stop, questioning and observations, including the field sobriety tests. The use of the test results from the taking of the breathalyzer test usually the ultimate culminating basis for the law enforcement officer to establish "probable cause" and then arrest the suspect on the charge of DWI. The breathalyzer machines commonly used in Louisiana is called the Intoxilyzer 5000 and the Intoxilyzer 9000 Breathalyzers. This most used machine, being the Intoxilyzer 5000, has a reported standard margin of error of 0.02 BAC which is significant enough to make a difference in many cases as to whether someone is presumed to have violated Louisiana DWI law or not.

The Louisiana law enforcement officer will tell the DWI suspect that they will have their driving privileges suspended unless they take the breathalyzer test. This is true; however, a highly skilled Louisiana DWI may be able to question whether or not the "refusal was, in fact, a legal refusal. Many considerations must be taken into consideration which can be discussed with your attorney. For example, not all breathalyzer samples that are taken where the police officer says you did not blow hard enough are considered refusals. What can be done about your driving privileges will be discussed in the driving privileges section of this book.

Many factors affect the accuracy or inaccuracy of the breathalyzer testing. Higher alcohol level results are received when the suspect has residual mouth alcohol that remains in the mouth tissues resulting in a false higher than true breath alcohol concentration (BAC) level. The breathalyzer testing sample should not be taken until 15 minutes after the suspect has consumed alcohol and/or has burped. Burping can also create a false reading. Tests can be contaminated and therefore not accurate if they are tainted by the introduction of substances such as cigarette smoke and chewing tobacco. Likewise, lower BAC results can occur when the sample is allowed to cool down before its analysis. Test results can also differ if breath from the mouth and upper area of the lungs combines with breath from deeper areas of the lungs. This is ultra-technical but provides further reasons why a very experienced DWI attorney may be able to defeat breathalyzer results attempted to be introduced by the prosecution.

The breathalyzer testing may be challenged by a competent DWI defense lawyer based errors, deficiencies, flaws in the law and fact, including but not limited to the following:

- The contents and source of breath used in testing
- The suspects medical and physical conditions
- Defects in the breathalyzer machine
- Lack of proper certification of the accuracy of the breathalyzer machine
- Lack of credentials of operator of breathalyzer machine
- Failure to use proper procedures in administering breathalyzer test, and
- The margin of error of the Intoxilizer 5000 or Intoxilizer 9000

The Louisiana Department of Public Safety and Corrections, known as the DPSC, has strict regulations regarding the Intoxilyzer 5000, which includes the following:

"At least once every four months thereafter for the Intoxilyzer 5000..., each individual instrument shall be inspected, checked, and certified by the applied technology director, breath analysis supervisor, breath analysis specialist, breath analysis instructor specialist, or applied technology specialist of the Applied Technology Unit and a recertification form shall be maintained in the Applies Technology Unit. A copy of this certificate may be filed with the clerk of the applicable court in the respective parish in which each device is used for blood/breath testing, and this copy shall be prima facie evidence as to the proper working order of the instrument."

Hence, the introduction of the results of an Intoxilyzer 5000 breath test is dependent upon proper inspection, testing, and certification of the machine. The Louisiana Supreme Court has guidelines regarding the validity of these chemical tests. The chemical testing required qualifications of operators, instructors, and maintenance technicians, with required scheduled maintenance and repairs, approved simulator solutions and procedures for using the Intoxilyzer 5000.

Simply put, preliminary breath testing has many areas where the results might be successfully attacked and defeated as unreliable in court. It also serves as a strong ally to the state prosecutor if left to be used at trial against an unrepresented DWI defendant or an uninformed criminal defense attorney.

If you are reading this book, chances are good that you or a loved one has gone through one or more of the above factual scenarios that lead to a law enforcement officer believing that he had probable cause to arrest the suspect for driving while intoxicated or driving under the influence as an impaired driver.

In many circumstances, if you refuse are unable to take a breathalyzer test, law enforcement may request a warrant to seek a blood test to determine your alcohol level.

Your DWI Arrest:

After the police officer has finished his investigative process, which may include the field sobriety testing and the breathalyzer testing, he will decide to release you from your detainment or arrest you for DWI. If arrested for DWI, the officer should read you your constitutional rights against self-incrimination which is commonly referred to as your Miranda rights. As experienced DWI attorneys, we always recommend that you never give a statement because at this point, after the arrest, the officer is only trying to gain further evidence for the State of Louisiana to use against you in the prosecution of you for driving while intoxicated. If you gave a statement, then you attorney will be entitled to receive a copy of it, as well as all other evidence. In certain instances, the statement and other potential evidence might be able to be surprised with motions and argument by your counsel.

Please keep in mind that the police officer will make an arrest report that includes all of the prior investigative methods referenced above as well as any spontaneous or voluntary statements that you make after your arrest and the reading of your Miranda rights to you. When placed into a police cruiser, at a booking facility or a testing facility, your statements and acts may be recorded and used against you.

Once you are placed in jail or a detention facility, you will need to see how to be released and seek competent legal representation.

Chapter 7

YOUR ARREST AND BAIL: The police arrested me for DWI: What's going to happen to me?

A Louisiana State Trooper, New Orleans Police Officer, Parish Sheriff's Deputy or other law enforcement officer has pulled you over and has arrested you for a first, second, third or subsequent DWI. What should you expect next?

When you are arrested in Louisiana for DWI or DUI, one of two things will occur:

1. You are arrested and required to post a bond, sign a "signature bond," get released from "jail overcrowding" or get released on your "own recognizance" pending the first scheduled court appearance; or

2. You are unable to post a bond and you will remain in jail until at least your first court date.

Posting bail means that you, a family member, a friend or a bail bonds company provides the Court with a money deposit or a lien on real estate to assure that you will appear at the various scheduled court appearances. Failure to appear at your scheduled court appearance could result in forfeiture of the bond and an attachment for your arrest for failure to appear when ordered to do so.

A Louisiana Judge, Magistrate or Criminal Commissioner

will set your bond depending on the nature and perceived severity of the charges against you, on your prior criminal history, on whether you are gainfully employed and whether you are a flight risk. Quite often, bail is set by a bail schedule based on the charges in which you were arrested on.

The three basis ways to post bail are as follows:

1. Provide sufficient cash or credit card charge to meet the bond requirements and post bond. (If you timely make all of your court appearances, your bond may be returned to you.);
2. Provide a Property or signature bond (If you timely make all of your court appearances the lien on the subject property may be lifted.); or
3. Hire a bail bonds person to post your bond for a premium fee. (Our law office can recommend well-known bail bond companies in the city or parish of your DWI Offense).

If you are not allowed or able to post a "reasonable" bond and are not released from jail after a DWI arrest, this may occur because of several reasons:

1. First, you simply may not be able to afford the current bond; in which case, your attorney may move and request for a reduction of the bond at a subsequent hearing;
2. You may be considered a non-resident and a flight risk. Here the Court is concerned that you may not return to the Louisiana Court for your hearings and trial.

3. You may have a serious criminal history or prior DWI arrests or convictions;
4. You may have caused an automobile accident wherein someone was injured or killed. In these cases, your bond may be expected to be very high.

You certainly need an experienced DWI attorney who practices in that city or parish when you or a loved one is unable to get out of jail on a DWI charge.

WARNING: When you are in jail, do not discuss the facts of the case with anyone: in jail (other than your attorney), during any visitation with any non-lawyer, or over the telephone, because quite often these communications are recorded by the jail, and any admissions can be used against you, unless the communication is between you and your attorney.

Your first court appearance is usually for a status hearing to determine your bail and/or for an arraignment. At or before your arraignment, the State of Louisiana prosecutor for that city or parish will file the charges against you, possibly modify your bail. The arraignment is the time when the Court asks you what your plea is…" Guilty or Not Guilty." Any experienced DWI lawyer will recommend that you should consider plea "Not Guilty" at the arraignment. You may change your plea later if desired. This will give you time to meet with your selected DWI attorney who should take time with you to discuss all aspects of the case.

Hopefully, you will be released from jail after the bond is set. At that time, it is extremely important that you hire the right experienced DWI Attorney who routinely practices in the parish where you received your DWI. Secondly, it's important that your take action, if necessary, to request an Administrative Hearing with the Louisiana Department of Motor Vehicles to preserve your immediate driving privileges. The form needed to request the administrative hearing was likely given to you upon your arrest or release from jail. There are strict time limitations on mailing out this form.

What will happen in your criminal DWI case and your Administrative hearing regarding your driving privileges may be significantly affected by whether or not you hire an experienced DWI lawyer. We shall discuss these topics in upcoming chapters of this book.

Chapter 8

Secrets to Hiring an Experienced DWI Attorney

When in the process of hiring a lawyer to represent you in your DWI case, please do your due diligence. Don't just hire the first criminal defense attorney you happen to stumble across on the internet, sends you a letter without providing his credentials or get referred to you by your relative. Spend time examining the attorney's website, references, testimonials, online reviews and accolades from groups like Avvo.com, Yelp.com, and BestAttorneysofAmerica.com. Has the attorney written any books or articles on Louisiana DWI defense? How many DWI cases has the lawyer represented? Does the attorney routinely represent DWI defendants in the Court where your charges are pending?

The great secrets to finding a great DWI attorney is doing your own due diligence and asking the right questions.

- Learn about the DWI lawyer's professional background and experience.
- One the attorney learns about the facts of your case, discuss with your potential lawyer the various potential options and possible strategies for your case.
- Is the lawyer a good match for you?

When you set up an appointment with your potential DWI defense attorney, bring with you all papers that you have been given regarding your arrest and court documents. Bring with you:

- Any court documents that sets out the charges against you and your next court date
- Your bond/bail documents
- The police report, if possible
- Any other documents that the police may have given you report
- Your Request for Hearing form regarding your driving privileges. (If you have not done so, please immediately fill out and mail out your Request for Hearing Form, as discussed in Chapter 11 of this book.

You should also create a list of all the names, addresses and telephone numbers of any witnesses connected to your DWI case.

Here are some questions that you may care to ask the lawyer:

- How long has he been practicing law?
- What percentage of his practice is dedicated to DWI defense?
- How many DWI clients has he represented?
- Has he ever been a DWI prosecutor before being a criminal defense attorney?
- Does he routinely represent DWI clients in the parish or city in which you received your DWI arrest?

- Does he only represent people charged with only first offense DWI or does he have valuable experience representing people charged with Second Offence DWI, Third Offense DWI, and other serious felony DWIs?
- Has the lawyer received any professional awards and been invited into membership in esteemed criminal defense attorney organizations?
- Has he ever written any books or publications on Louisiana DWI?
- Who will be my primary attorney?
- Do they work as a team of more than one experienced attorneys at the same flat fee?
- Based on the facts of my case, what does he think my options are?
- How often do you appear at the court where my case will be conducted?
- Have you previously negotiated with or gone to trial againt the prosecuting attorney in my case?
- Do you generally negotiate plea agreements?
- How often do you represent people in DUI or DWI cases to trial?
- How does payment work?
- Does he have payment plans?
- What distinguishes the firm and makes it unique?
- How often will my attorney communicate with me in person or on the telephone?
- Does the attorney have clients who have provided testimonials praising the lawyer's DWI representation abilities and results?

Your lawyer needs to learn the detailed facts of your case. After he is sufficiently informed, discuss whwther you should enter a plea bargain or tgo to trial. You should ask how ofetn you will communicate with your attorney and fully prepare for trial , if there is one

Legal Fees

You can determine what your legal fees will be once you talk to your potential DWI lawyer. When you are considering whether or not the fees are too high, remember that there is a reason why some lawyers charge more, many are simply worth it. As you consider costs, apply the same thinking process. If you need a heart transplant, would you look for the *cheapest* cardiologist money can buy? Probably not! The stakes are too high, and the consequences of a bad job or even a mediocre one are too grave to risk. Likewise, the consequences of a negative result on your DWI offense can have great repercussions that can last for years or decades. They might include ample jail time, loss of your license, the torpedoing of your career, problems with your divorce or child custody negotiations, spikes on your insurance rate and more.

Most Louisiana DWI lawyers charge a flat fee for DWI representation. Many lawyers now accept credit cards for payment of fees.

Hiring Your DWI Lawyer

After interviewing DWI lawyers, choose the most qualified attorney. As the candidates to be your lawyer for the names and contact information for a few former clients. Call them to get some first-hand feedback, including recommendations and critiques.

Find an attorney whose *values* resonate with your own. You will likely need to work with this person on a very intimate level. You want to trust that he or she believes in you and your case and has the skills, resources and time to deliver a powerful strategic defense.

If you still are unsure, please feel free to call the Author of this book, DWI Attorney Stephen Rue and he will be available to discuss your case with you.

DWI Attorney Stephen Rue
(504)529-5000
(985)871-0008
StephenRue.com
Rue@StephenRue.com

Chapter 9

Your DWI Defense

Your very best DWI defense of the charges against you start with your choice of the attorney that you hire. That attorney should be a fully competent and experienced DWI in the court where you DWI charge is pending.

Please do not fail to consider hiring a lawyer to represent you. Once arrested for DWI, some people simply give up and a plea to the DWI and related offenses as charges. An arrest does not guarantee a conviction. You are presumed innocent until proven otherwise. Please speak to an experienced DWI attorney to weigh your options.

Please also remember that when arrested for DWI in Louisiana, you also will have to address your driving privileges with the State. Please immediately fill out and mail in your **REQUEST FOR HEARING** regarding your driving privileges **within 15 days of your DWI arrest**. Your DWI criminal defense lawyer also may be able to asset you with your driving privileges. Please see our Chapter 11 regarding these issues.

Your experienced attorney should be fully prepared to provide you the very best legal services for you. Of course, the goal is to maximize your results in the DWI criminal proceeding and the Administrative Hearing regarding your driving privileges. The best results possible are affected by the facts of the case, the quality of the police investigation, the evidence against you, the exculpatory evidence, the applicable law, whether your case is to be heard by a jury or judge trial and the quality of your DWI defense counsel.

There are five general categories of attack of evidence in a DWI case; they are the following:

1. Driving
3. The Drivers appearance and demeanor
4. The Field sobriety tests
5. The Driver's statements
6. The Chemical tests

You capable DWI defense should attack all of these general categories of evidence. Likewise your criminal defense attorney should attack the investigating police officer's perceptions regarding the initial vehicle stop, initial interview, and Pre-Miranda questioning, field sobriety testing, Chemical testing procedures, attacking the accuracy of breathalyzerer, DWI checkpoint, if applicable, arrest procedure, post-arrest statements, interviews of other witnesses, digital video and recordings, Officer's prior training and certification, or lack thereof, officer's memory, flaws in the incident reporting, technical flaws required by law.

Your DWI Attorney's Defense Strategy

Depending on the factual circumstances of your particular case, your DWI lawyer may attack many of the allegations, facts, positions, opinions, protocol, procedures, certifications, test results and more of the following:

1. The "Reasonable Cause" for the initial vehicle stop
2. Facts associated with the law enforcement officer approaching the vehicle
3. Facts regarding the DWI Checkpoint Stop / "Sobriety Checkpoint, if any
4. The observations of the alleged impaired driver by the law enforcement officer
5. The personal contact with the driver behind the wheel
6. The initial questioning and answers while the driver in the vehicle
7. The exiting sequence of the driver
8. Pre-Miranda Questioning (Before being read rights against self-incrimination)
9. Medical Questioning
10. Questioning regarding the location site for the Standardized Field Sobriety Tests
11. Questioning regarding the location site for any non-standardized Field Sobriety Tests
12. Questions regarding Officer's training and qualifications as to Field Sobriety Testing
13. Attacking the Horizontal Gaze Nystagmus Testing, Procedures and the non-alcohol or drug related medical or physical conditions of the driver that could affect test results or conclusions
14. Attacking the Walk & Turn Testing, Procedures and the non-alcohol or drug-related the medical or physical conditions of the driver that could affect the test results or conclusions
15. Attacking the "One-Leg Stand" Testing, Procedures and the non-alcohol or drug-related the medical or physical conditions of the driver that could affect the test results or conclusions
16. Addressing the coordination and balance issues of the

driver and the non-alcohol or drug related the medical or physical conditions of the driver that could affect the test results or conclusions

17. Addressing any perception that the driver had red eyes and the non-alcohol or drug related medical or physical conditions of the driver that could affect the test results or conclusions
18. Addressing any perception that the driver smelled of the odor of alcohol the non-impaired driver reasons why the driver that have had the odor of alcohol or similar odor
19. Questioning regarding the verbal command/instructions and demonstrations associated with each field sobriety test requested
20. Addressing the inaccuracies of the "Romberg" Field Sobriety Testing Procedure
21. Addressing the inaccuracies of the finger to nose procedure
22. Addressing the inaccuracies and lack of direct correlation between counting the alphabet or numbers backward as it relates to being impaired
23. Address the issue of whether the driver understood the instructions, directions, and demonstrations of the investigation officer regarding field sobriety tests
24. Questioning the procedures used, training and experience of the officer administrating the preliminary breath testing (Breathalyzer)
25. Questioning the certification of the officer administrating the preliminary breath testing (Breathalyzer)
26. Questioning the admonitions used by the officer to the driver in administrating the preliminary breath testing (Breathalyzer)

27. Question the certification of the officer administrating the preliminary breath testing (Breathalyzer)
28. Question the certification of the actual preliminary breath testing machine (Breathalyzer)
29. Question the timing of the breath testing machine by the officer of the driver from the time of first continual observation, without the suspect burping, vomiting or consuming anything
30. Investigation and questioning regarding the probable cause affidavit associated with obtaining a warrant for blood sampling
31. Questioning regarding the warrant for blood testing
32. Questioning the process of taking the blood sample and the subsequent chain of custody and testing of that blood sample
33. Full inquiries as to all State prosecution witnesses
34. Full inquiry with all defense witnesses
35. Full inquiry with all expert witnesses, if any
36. Attacking the credibility and bias of the investigation officer and any other state witness
37. Questioning the decision to arrest
38. Inquiries as to the actual arrest
39. Statements of the Driver before the Miranda Constitutional reading of rights
40. Statements of the driver after the Miranda Constitutional rights from is read
41. Any spontaneous statements of the driver
42. Review and questioning regarding the Preliminary Investigative Report
43. Review and questioning regarding officer notes used to create Preliminary Instigative Report
44. Review and questioning regarding any associated reports such as supervisor shift report, pursuit report,

traffic citation report, accident narrative, chemical admonition form, Miranda rights waiver form, evidence report, vehicle inspection and storage report, DMV notification form, reports prepared by other law enforcement officers, radio dispatch recordings, use of force form, injury report, medical records, jail pre-booking form, jail booking form, and any and all digital or video recording of driver.
45. Review and Questioning as to Resume and credentials of investigating officer
46. Attacking any and all incriminating, flawed, inaccurate or unreliable perceptions, observations, opinions, bias, flaws, procedures, techniques, testing, and/or suggested evidence of any nature and kind.

The varied ways in which you DWI lawyer can assist you and provide a valuable defense to the charges against you have been more fully addressed in each chapter of this book. For the sake of brevity, they will not be restated here. Additionally, what should help in your defense is your attorney's litigation abilities as well as his ethical professional relationship with the prosecuting attorney, that prosecutor's supervisor, and the court. Ultimately, at the end of the day, after through discussions with your attorney, after various motions and hearings have been resolved, the decision must be made whether to enter into a pre-trial diversionary program, plea as charged, enter a "plea bargain," or go to trial.

Chapter 10

To Enter a Plea or Go to Trial

If charged with DWI, one of several options may occur, including but not limited to the following:

1. The State of Louisiana dismisses the charges (Seldom occurs);
2. The Court enters a finding of technical or legal error associated with stop, arrest, investigation, and/or State's evidence resulting in the State's inability to effectively prosecute (Infrequent. Generally, as a result of a good DWI defense motions and hearings);
3. The Defendant is accepted, enters and successfully completes a pre-trial diversionary program (Discussed in Chapter 12);
4. The Defendant enters a plea "as charged" by the State;
5. The Defendant enters a "plea bargain;" or
6. The Defendant goes to trial, by judge or jury depending on if misdemeanor or felony DWI.

The strength and weakness of the case facts, evidence, and the abilities of your defense attorney will determine your best options under your circumstances. Each case is different, this is why you should immediately hire an experience DWI attorney who is a true defender of your rights.

Chapter 11

The Louisiana DMV and Your Driving Privileges:

I need to drive for work, but I got a DWI.
Am I going to be out of a job?
Will my driver's license be suspended?
Can I get a Hardship or Restricted License?

Why You Need to Deal with Your Driving Privileges Immediately

A driver arrested for DWI certainly has to be concerned about the DWI criminal proceeding and the accused will have a scheduled upcoming court date; however, immediate attention must be given to your driving one's driving privileges which may be suspended as soon as 30 days after the arrest. This chapter will address those concerns and the actions that should be taken.

Louisiana Implied Consent Laws

Louisiana considers operating a vehicle on public streets or highways as a "privilege" and not a "right." Under what is known as the Louisiana implied consent law, it is illegal for a non-commercial driver to operate a vehicle on a Vehicle on Louisiana public streets or highways with a blood alcohol concentration (BAC) level of 0.08 percent or greater. Commercial drivers violate the law if they operate a vehicle with a blood alcohol concentration (BAC) level of 0.04 percent or greater.

"Implied consent," as the term suggests, mandates that an operator of a vehicle in Louisiana has implicitly consented to testing of the driver's alcohol level or for the existence of drugs as controlled dangerous substances. Additionally, a driver's refusal to submit to a breathalyzer, blood or urine test can result in one's suspension of their driving "privileges."

Refusal to Submit to Chemical Test

Louisiana Revises Statute 32:666 is the primary law governing a driver's refusal to submit to a chemical test. (See this law **www.LouisianaDWILaw.com** or **www.StephenRue.com**.)

The law is quite complex, and it is highly recommended that you immediately seek the counsel of an experienced DWI attorney to assist you in this separate but related proceeding to the DWI criminal proceeding. Louisiana law regarding refusal to submit to chemical tests associated with an arrest for DWI is quite complicated, and you should immediately seek the legal advice of an experienced DWI attorney as for how the law affects you.

To briefly summarize a few aspects of LA R.S. 32:666, Louisiana law provides that when a law enforcement officer has probable cause to believe that a person has operated a vehicle while intoxicated, that person may not refuse to submit to a chemical test or tests; if he has refused to submit to such test or tests on two previous and separate occasions of any previous such violation or in any case wherein a fatality has occurred, or a person has sustained serious bodily injury in a crash involving a motor vehicle, aircraft, watercraft, vessel, or other means of conveyance. The police may direct that a chemical test or tests be conducted of a person's blood, urine, or other bodily substance, or perform a chemical test of such person's breath, for the purpose of determining the alcoholic content of his blood and the presence of any abused substance or controlled substance in his blood. A refusal of any such test or tests shall result in the suspension of driving privileges. Additionally, any person who refuses to submit to a chemical test as required by law shall be fined not less than three hundred dollars nor more than one thousand dollars and imprisoned for not less than ten days nor more than six months. Imposition or execution of sentence shall not be suspended unless the offender is placed on probation with a minimum condition that he serve two days in jail and participate in a court-approved substance abuse program and participate in a court-approved driver improvement program; or the offender is placed on probation with a minimum condition that he perform four eight-hour days of court-approved community service activities, at least half of which shall consist of participation in a litter abatement or collection program, participate in a court-approved substance abuse program, and participate in a court-approved driver improvement program. In all cases other than those circumstances referred to above, a person under arrest for a violation of operating a vehicle while intoxicated may refuse to submit to such chemical test or tests, after being advised of the consequences of such refusal subject to the following: That his driver's license shall be seized; if he is a resident without a license or permit to operate a motor vehicle in this state, the department shall deny the issuance of a license or permit to such person for a period of six months after the date of the alleged violation; and evidence of his refusal shall be admissible in any criminal action or proceeding arising out of acts alleged to have been committed while the person, regardless of age, was driving or in actual physical control of a motor vehicle upon the public highways of this state while under the influence of alcoholic beverages or any abused substance or controlled dangerous substances.

Request for Administrative Hearing to Contest Suspension of Driving Privileges

In Louisiana, if you are arrested for DWI, you will also be dealing with the Department of Motor Vehicles regarding a potential suspension of your driver's license and driving privileges. This is a separate administrative proceeding; your driving privileges are in jeopardy. When a driver is released from jail after being arrested for suspicion of DWI, the driver is given various documents. One of these papers should be entitled **"REQUEST FOR HEARING."**

Should you wish to contest a suspension of your driving privileges, it is very important that you complete the **"REQUEST FOR HEARING"** form and mail the completed form to the Louisiana Department of Public Safety and Corrections, Office of Motor Vehicles **within fifteen (15) calendar date from the date of arrest**. (Recent Request for Hearing forms say you have 30 days, but the law says 15 days; therefore, don't chance it; get your "Request for Hearing" form mailed in immediately. This form is a request for an administrative hearing regarding your driving privileges. Your DWI lawyer may assist you at this hearing. Make sure that this is part of your lawyer's scope of representation when he is retained.

The mailing address to mail the form is as follows:

**Louisiana Department of Public Safety and Corrections
Office of Motor Vehicles
P.O. Box 64886
Baton Rouge, LA 70896-4886**

(Please check your form as the State of Louisiana may have changed to form return address since the recent publication date of this book.)

For information from the State regarding obtaining a hardship license or more information regarding a request for a hearing, you may call the Office of Motor Vehicles at **1-(225) 925-6146.**

Unfortunately, with a recent change in the law, under Louisiana Revised Statute 32:668 (A), no law enforcement officer shall be compelled by you to appear or testify at the administrative hearing. This means that an accused driver can no longer subpoena the investigating police officer who made the arrest or who requested that you submit to a chemical test.

Request a Hardship or Restricted License

If a Louisiana driver's license is suspended as a result of a DWI arrest, the driver may request a restricted or hardship license which generally requires that n ignition interlock system is installed in the driver's vehicle. This device requires the driver to blow into the machine to start the vehicle and other times during the drive. The ignition interlock device is designed to ensure that the driver does not operate the vehicle while under the influence of alcohol. It was be leased and installed by a court approved installer and monitor.

If granted a hardship or restricted license by your DWI court, you likely will be restricted as to the time and purpose of driving such as going to and from work and other tasks permitted by the Court.

Commercial Drivers

The implied consent law that applies to **commercial drivers** is Louisiana Revised Statute 32:414.2. A full copy of the statute is found at **www.LouisianaDWILaw.com**. The requirements and penalties are more severe for commercial drivers. A commercial driver's minimum BAC is 0.04 percent or above to allow a suspension. A first suspension is for one year; a second suspension is for life. The financial implications are great. Thus a talented, hiring an experienced DWI attorney is quite prudent for any commercial driver who is charged with a DWI.

Non-Resident Drivers

If you are not a resident of Louisiana, who refuses an approved chemical test the Louisiana Department of Public Safety and Corrections shall notify the state's motor vehicle administrator of the driver's residence in which he has a license. (Please see Louisiana Revised

Statue 32:669 and other helpful information at **www.LouisianaDWILaw.com.**

Chapter 12

Clearing Your DWI Record

Pre-Trial Diversion Programs Throughout Louisiana

Some Courts throughout Louisiana allow first time DWI arrestees to participate in what is commonly known as a "Pre-Trial Diversion Program." Not all of the DWI Courts have these programs, and they vary in scope, cost, and intensity from venue to venue. In these cases, applicants who qualify for the particular program may avoid a First Offense DWI conviction by fully completing and satisfying the strict and often expensive requirement of the program. Some programs may last just a few months, while other may last over two years.

Please note that the DWI charges will remain pending subject to the program participant's full completion of the program satisfying the requirements of the Court. If the District Attorney's Office agrees that there has been a successful completion of the Pre-Trial Diversion Program, then the pending charges may be dismissed, without any conviction for the First Offense DWI.

It is very important to know that anyone who is considering accepting an offer to participate in a Pre-Trial Diversion Program, that they should be dedicated financially and to all requirements of the program, including not committing another crime. Some common requirements include the following:

Most Courts require an intense alcohol and drug assessment and for the participant to comply with the suggested terms of substance abuse treatment. Courts with the programs include parish community service programs, random drug, and/or alcohol testing/screening. required attendance at Alcoholics Anonymous (AA) or Narcotics Anonymous (NA) meetings, required attendance to one or more M.A.D.D. victim impact courses, completion of driver's improvement classes. requirement of ignition interlock device in defendant's vehicle, "Probationary" or "Monitoring" Fees, as well as any other requirements of the Pre-Trial Diversion Program. It is quite a task intended to ensure that the Courts have a reasonable degree of comfort that the alleged substance abuse issue is behind the defendant.

If the participate violates one or more conditions of the program, then he or she may be revoked from the program and thus have the pending DWI charges be actively pursued against the DWI defendant.

Louisiana Code of Criminal Procedure Articles 894 and 893

When you are arrested for the first time on DWI, you will inevitably hear something about Article 984. Many people have to wrong idea of what it is and what it is not. In certain circumstances, if a defendant pleads guilty to a misdemeanor DWI under the provisions of Louisiana Code of Civil Procedure Article 894 (Commonly referred to as "under Article 894" for misdemeanors) and the defendant has successfully completed the terms plea agreement of paying fines and costs as well as inactive conviction (without any other conviction within 10 years), then the defendant can go back to Court and have a Motion to Set Aside the plea and for dismiss the defendant's case. Subsequent to the set aside motion being granted, the defendant can then move for an expungement of the record. Please do not mistakenly believe that someone who pleads under Article 894 automatically receives an expungement of the record as this is not the case. A separate subsequent Motion for Expungement must be filed and granted by the Court to have a successful expungement of the record (To be discussed below). Louisiana Code of Criminal Procedure 893 relates to felony pleas and has strict requirements. (Please see selected laws are at **www.LouisianaDWILaw.com** and at **www.StephenRue.com** as the changes in the laws are updated on the author/attorney websites changes occur.)

Expungement of Record

The process of clearing your public record of any DWI charge is commonly known as an "Expungement." Louisiana expungement law is complex and should not be considered as a "given," insofar as whether a conviction can be expunged is largely based on Louisiana statutes. You should discuss your desire for an expungement early in your attorney's representation of you so that each of you is clear on whether an expungement may be a possibility. Under the specific facts of your case, you may desire a more favorable plea bargain that may permit your DWI to be expunged from the public record.

It is important for you to understand that an expungement does not prohibit the State from using a prior DWI conviction as a predicate offense for a second, third or subsequent DWI offense.

In many instances, a judge will not permit an expungement until there has been a lapse of time without further DWI or criminal offenses.

Take action to protect your freedom

I want to thank you again for choosing to spend time with me – to hear my perspective on DUI, reckless driving and speeding charges.

Hopefully, this brief primer has been helpful, but I'm guessing that you're likely still concerned or confused about aspects of your case. You might greatly benefit from speaking with me about how to move forward.

For a typical consultation, I normally charge $250. But I would like to offer you, as a thank you gift for reading this book, a FREE initial consultation. Just mention that you read this book when you call our offices today at **(504)529-5000 or (985)871-0008**.

You *can* regain control of your situation and not only recover from your charges but also become a better, more confident driver and citizen. Please take advantage of this special offer, and book your free consultation now. I look forward to helping you!

Sincerely,

Stephen Rue

Stephen Rue
Attorney-at-Law

ABOUT THE AUTHOR
Attorney Stephen Rue

Stephen Rue is a very experienced DWI attorney who has a tremendous support team. He and his legal team which, includes a former Assistant District Attorney who previously prosecuted hundreds of DWI cases, has over 30 years of intense experience in representing persons charged with First Offence DWI, Second Offense DWI, Third and Fourth Offense DWI, and related serious traffic related offenses throughout Louisiana. Stephen Rue and his other experienced attorneys are available to assist you or a loved one in criminal defense representation. Stephen Rue & Associates have several offices throughout the Greater New Orleans Area, including New Orleans, Gretna, Kenner, and Covington. Call to speak with Attorney Stephen Rue at (504)529-5000 or (985)871-0008.

Mr. Rue is a highly-respected trial lawyer, author, and lecturer. Stephen Rue is honored by being selected the **"BEST ATTORNEY"** in Gambit Weekly's Best of New Orleans Readers Poll (2012). Rue was selected for inclusion within **"Louisiana Super Lawyers 2017."** Stephen has a **"SUPERB"** 10 out of 10 Rating by AVVO Attorney Ratings, Rue received the AVVO Client's Choice Award in 2014 in the field of Criminal Law. Stephen Rue is honored by **the National Trial Lawyers Top 100 Lawyer Award for 2016 Criminal Lawyers**. Rue received the National Association of Criminal Defense Attorneys (NACDA) **"2015 National Ranked Top Ten Attorney Awards for Excellence in the Field of Criminal Defense."** Rue is also honored is honored by receiving the **National Association of Distinguished Counsel's (NADC) Nation Top One Percent Award in 2015.** Stephen Rue is a 2017 member of the **American Association of Premier DUI Attorneys**. Rue continues to receive many 5 Star Yelp reviews from his clients. Stephen Rue is a **Fellow of the National Institute of Trial Advocacy**. Rue has lectured to associations, attorneys and law students on issues regarding various trial litigation skills and techniques. Stephen Rue's awards and invitations to membership in prestigious legal organizations grows yearly.

The esteem most appreciated by Stephen Rue is that received by the praise of his clients. You can review his client testimonials at his law firm's websites at **StephenRue.com** and **LouisianaDUILaw.com**

You are invited to contact Attorney Stephen Rue and his team of experienced attorneys at **(504)529-5000** or **(985)871-0008.** The telephone is answered 24 hours a day, seven days a week.

Experienced DWI/DUI Defense

Call our law office today:
Stephen Rue & Associates

www.StephenRue.com
Make your appointment for a
**FREE 30-MINUTE
DWI INITIAL CONSULTATION**

For more information, please contact:
**Stephen Rue & Associates
Law Offices by Appointment**

Gretna Law Office
422 Derbigny Street
Gretna, LA 70053

New Orleans Law Office
1100 Poydras Street, Ste. 2900
New Orleans, LA 70163

Covington Law Office
416 N. Vermont Street
Covington, LA 70433

Kenner Law Office
3309 Williams Blvd.
Kenner, LA 70065

Metairie Law Office
1 Galleria Blvd,, Ste 1900
Metairie, LA 70001

**(504)529-5000
(985)871-0008**
Contact the author directly at: **Rue@StephenRue.com**
Selected Louisiana DWI Laws are found at:
**www.LouisianaDWILaw.com
www.StephenRue.com**

www.ingramcontent.com/pod-product-compliance
Lightning Source LLC
Chambersburg PA
CBHW070120210526
45170CB00013B/833